cheam village

past and present

Comparative views
from

1891~1991

Frank Burgess

Published by Sutton Leisure Services

FOREWORD

It gives me great pleasure to be able to publish a fourth book by Frank Burgess, who has done so much to illuminate the history of our local area over the last twenty years.

Frank came to the district as a local government engineer in 1938, and over the years was personally involved in many of the changes which have taken place in our environment and are recorded in these pages.

His interest in the history of the area grew and he began to collect old photographs, which marked the beginning of a unique collaboration between Sutton Leisure Services and this talented photographer and amateur historian. The local history illustrations collection and archives were initially the source of Frank's collection of old views of the borough, and has gained from his researches and the many photographs lent to him for copying by local residents.

Library staff persuaded Frank to give slide lectures, where he showed old and contemporary views side by side and shared his discoveries with fascinated audiences. This led eventually to his first book *Old Cheam*, which was published by Sutton Libraries in 1978. By popular request two more books of comparative views of the Sutton area followed, and now Frank has been persuaded to delight us once more with a book concentrating on the Cheam Village area, showing the changes that have taken place over the last century.

It is hard to envisage today the rural village that Cheam once was, but this book provides the information needed to make that leap of imagination back to a time still within the living memory of older residents, to a more restful age where life moved at a different pace. So much has changed in Cheam that Frank's guidance is necessary to recognise many of the old views. However time has passed by some buildings - in particular Whitehall, which is now in the care of Sutton Leisure Services and open to the public - without leaving a visible trace and these will be greeted with pleasure by all who are familiar with present-day Cheam.

I am sure that this book will prove as popular as his previous volumes with all who have an interest in our borough's heritage, particularly in the Cheam area.

Peter Smithson
Director of Leisure Services, London Borough of Sutton

October 1991

First published 1991.   c Frank Burgess 1991

London Borough of Sutton Leisure Services, The Old Court House, Throwley Way, Sutton, Surrey, SM1 4AF

Printed by Dicker & Dunster (Printers) Ltd, Mitcham, Surrey.

INTRODUCTION

In 1978 I compiled a book of old photographs of Cheam, which proved very popular and is now out of print. However, copies are still available for loan from Sutton Public Libraries. As there is still a demand for retail copies of such a book I have been urged to compile a second version, this time including present day photographs, matching the old views to enable identification to be made easily.

In the case of Cheam, development of the Village as we know it today has taken place in the last 70 years, so it is well within the period of outdoor photography, and, indeed, within the lives of many present-day residents. It is from these two facts that I have derived my extensive knowledge of the recent history of the district, as I only came to reside here in 1938. Since 1972, I have given over 360 slide shows, and members of audiences have very generously turned up with their treasured old photographs and lent them to me to copy, with the result that I have now nearly 2,000 negatives of Sutton and Cheam.

This enables me to include photographs not previously published, but at the same time creates the great problem of selection. As before, I approached this on the basis of, first, rarity; secondly, interest; and thirdly, but not least, of reproduction quality. In this I was greatly helped by my friend June Broughton, Assistant Heritage Officer; and I hope our choice has included ones which will interest everyone, from old Cheam residents who may be reminded of their childhood, to new and younger residents interested in the history of our village.

I offer no apologies for having included a number of near-similar views of some locations, as this helps one to fix the atmosphere of the old village in one's mind.

In my books on Sutton with old and new views, I was able, in most cases, to include in both views an item common to both, which left no doubt as to the location. In this new book on Cheam, the aim was the same; but over the period concerned the village has changed so much that, in many cases, nothing remains to include in the modern view. I can, however, assure the reader that great care has been taken to get the positioning correct.

In *Old Cheam*, I included a fair amount of historical comment. In this book, where the old views are accompanied by a present day (1991) view of the same spot, I mainly leave the photographs to speak for themselves, only making sufficient comment to help with their identification.

ACKNOWLEDGEMENTS

As in the case of my previous books, the old photographs are reproduced from the large collection which has been gathered together with the generous help of the many owners of original photographs, postcards and other old prints. Those in the Sutton Heritage collection are used with the permission of the Director of Leisure Services, Peter Smithson, for which I am most grateful. They were made available to me by the willing and helpful co-operation of June Broughton, Assistant Heritage Officer, without whose help I could not have carried out the work.

These are friends and colleagues who are still with us, but I am sure they would agree with me that we are all indebted to the people of the past: firstly the old photographers who took and printed such superb examples of their art; then the owners who have preserved them over the years; and finally the present owners who have made them available to us. To all of these I acknowledge with gratitude my indebtedness. In addition, I apologise to anyone whose picture I may have used without their specific permission.

I also extend my grateful thanks to George Jenkinson, F.R.P.S., for his competent processing of my modern photographs. In addition, I would like to extend my appreciation and sincere thanks to Peter Smithson for writing the foreword to this volume. Finally, I would like to express my gratitude to the designer, Shirley Edwards, another friend and until recently a member of staff of Sutton Leisure Services, for the pleasing presentation of this book. My sincere thanks to them all.

F.B.
Cheam, 1991

Cheam Court Farmhouse on the south-west corner of the village crossroads in 1928. It is interesting to speculate for what traffic the point-duty policeman is holding up the chap on the tradesman's delivery cycle.

The site of Cheam Court Farmhouse, with Station Way to the left and Ewell Road to the right. The flats above the shops, Cheam Court, commemorate the name of the farm.

Old Brewery, Cheam. C475.

A view at the crossroads prior to 1920, looking north along Malden Road, now The Broadway, but at one period called Station Road. Another old photograph with a policeman on duty: in this case, the constable has his back to the corner building of Cheam Brewery, which was in production until 1902.

Although there is nothing of the old scene still visible in this matching view, there is an invisible relic still in existence: the cellars of the brewery building still survive beneath the grass triangles on which the tree is growing.

The clue to identifying this view is the wooden finger-post, which stood on the north-east corner of the crossroads. We are therefore looking across the foot of High Street to The Plough public house, on which one can just see the word 'STOUT'. The house in the centre of the picture was the earlier Plough.

The same location today. The Plough stood where the grass plots now are, outside Graham Andrews' tailor's and Coombe's baker's shops. The absence of the earlier Plough reveals the Harrow Inn.

CHEAM HOUSE

This is Cheam House, not to be confused with Cheam Park House. This large mansion stood across what is now Parkside, behind the Midland Bank.

The entrance gate and railings of Cheam House, shown in the old photograph, stood where the centre line now is, in front of the Old Cottage; evidence of a much-widened Broadway.

Cheam Park House in 1928. This lovely building was severely damaged by a flying-bomb in 1944, and completely cleared away after the war.

I am often asked where the old house stood: this view answers the question.

Two policemen at the crossroads this time, and a clear view of the brewery corner in 1921. The posters on the wall tell us that the brewery is about to be demolished and that second-hand building materials will be for sale. The posters are dated 1920. The sign of The Plough is on the public house which stood on the south-east corner, and belonged to Cheam Brewery. It was demolished in the early 1930s.

Time has changed the view, not least in the absence of policemen, who have been replaced by traffic signals.

The crossroads in about 1910, looking up High Street, with the brewery building on the extreme left of the picture, and The Plough public house on the right. This is a rare view of the crossroads without a police constable on duty.

The brewery has gone; likewise The Plough, which, according to Charles Marshall in his *History of Cheam and Sutton*, was demolished and replaced by one of the same name in Gander Green Lane in 1935.

The foot of High Street, c.1920, when Norrington's three-storey building stood on the corner of Malden Road, and The Plough, right, on the corner of Station Road. The small 'shop' to the right of Norrington's was the first branch of Barclays' Bank in Cheam.

In the old view, the 'Harrow' sign can be seen beyond The Plough; here, the new Harrow stands on the old site, and The Plough site is occupied by the grass triangles.

The same view as in the previous pair of photographs, taken in 1954. The undeveloped frontages at that date will surprise many readers, but the concrete lamp standards give it away.

37 years of change.

This view of the bottom of High Street in 1912 shows the little draper's shop between The Plough and The Harrow, with the name W.D. Harris over the shop window. This became Percy Harris's first shop when he came to Cheam in 1927 (Percy Harris's is still a well-known shop in Cheam today, now run by Percy's son). It is an interesting coincidence that their names were the same, though they were quite unrelated. In between W.D. and Percy Harris, the shop was owned by Mr. E. Shackleton (see page 62).

The Plough and the little shop were demolished in the early 1930s. New buildings were erected in Station Way at this time, and Percy Harris moved into the shop which still bears his name today.

This is an interesting photograph of the Harrow Inn, as it shows the back of the new pub being built at the rear of the old one, before its demolition.

The roof and chimney-stack at the rear of the Harrow in this view can be recognised as the half-built portion in the old picture. It also indicates how much higher the new building is than the old one.

To many residents of Cheam this picture will recall vivid memories, as it was the last of the old village buildings to go. It stood on the north side of High Street, and was demolished about 1970.

This is what replaced it; I will say no more!

A view looking down High Street to the old Harrow Inn at the bottom in 1925. The building on the left-hand side was demolished in 1934 (see page 30) when the road was widened.

An entirely different scene, the Harrow Inn being the only anchor point, and, significantly, not a tree remaining.

High Street, when it was so narrow that a double-decker bus and a car could only just pass. The demolition of the cottage suggests that the photograph was taken in 1934, in preparation for the widening of the street.

Although the clearance of the south side of the street took place in 1934, it remained vacant land until the late 1950s.

High Street, with Ebbutt's, landscape gardener's and undertaker's, on the corner of Red Lion Street, now Park Road. The old Harrow Inn is visible at the bottom of the hill.

Truelove and Son have taken the place of the earlier undertaker; the modern colonnaded building has replaced the old cottages; and the new Harrow is visible at the foot of the hill.

The Cheam School building for sale in 1934, and evidence that the widening of the road in front had already started. It was the loss of frontage land and trees that finally precipitated the school's move to Headley, near Newbury, in Berkshire.

Tabor Court, on the site of the old Cheam School.

The White House, which stood in High Street opposite Cheam School. It was pulled down in the late 1930s for private redevelopment, but the war interrupted the project, and after V.E. Day the site was taken over by Sutton and Cheam Council. Farnham Court was built, in a style which would not disgrace Tudor Court, across the road.

Farnham Court forty years later.

Cheam School playground in 1903, showing the school chapel on the left-hand side.

The rear of Tabor Court, showing not only the chapel building, now St. Christopher's Roman Catholic Church, but also the leaning tree, on the left in the old view, still in good heart.

This shows the Old Cottage in its original position in Malden Road (now The Broadway) in 1922, immediately prior to its dismantling for re-erection further back and a little way northwards, where it is today.

On this matching view I have shown in dotted lines the original location of the cottage, derived from evidence in old plans and photographs.

This is another view which shows the Old Cottage in its original position. It also shows the stagger in the crossroads, with the Plough public house on the very corner of Station Way.

I have shown here in dotted lines, as I did on page 41, the original position of the Old Cottage. The stagger of the crossroads still exists today, although less severe.

Malden Road, before it was widened and renamed The Broadway in 1934. The Old Cottage is in its new position, and the modern buildings have been built beyond it on both sides of the road.

The buildings on the left-hand side can be recognised, but Old Cottage is obscured by the large building on the far corner of Parkside, occupied for many years by Messrs. Sainsbury's Cheam branch.

'Necton', an attractive house of character, which stood in The Broadway. The ground floor was originally the kitchen-garden bothy and fruit store of Cheam House estate, but in the 1930s a Mr. Catton bought it, added the first floor and furnished the whole as a residence.

In the old view the black double-gates opened on to a drive which led to a house at the rear, which for many years was a doctor's surgery, and the ungated drive is still there today (1991).

This house, on the corner of Park Road and The Broadway, was called White Lodge (not to be confused with White House or Whitehall). On the right of the picture the Parochial Rooms can be seen.

White Lodge was demolished about 1965, when this modern block was built. Development of land obscures the contours of the ground, and it is not easy to see that the nearby St. Dunstan's Church stands on the highest point around; but this fact is confirmed from the top-storey windows of this block, where one can get a spectacular view of Epsom Grandstand on the downs.

Malden Road, from Whitehall to the Rectory, in 1925.

The road has been widened, traffic markings laid down and modern street-lighting installed; otherwise, little has changed.

The war memorial in the 1920s, shortly after it was erected. The stone seats and the field gun were part of the architect's design, but the village people so resented the inclusion of the gun, particularly as it turned out to be a German field gun, that one night the local youths trundled it round the corner to Springclose Lane, and tossed it down into the old Cheam Brickworks sandpit!

The site in 1991 with Cheam Branch Library on the site of the gun, and the trees almost obscuring the church.

Old St. Dunstan's Church, from a watercolour dated 1798, showing some of the ancient tombstones. This building was demolished in 1865.

The Lumley Chapel, which can be seen to be the chancel of the old church, with the clearly identifiable east window and the two box tombs, one exposed in the foreground, and the other, ivy-covered, nearer the chapel.

This is the yard and buildings of Church Farm, which lay behind the Farm House, which for many years afterwards was the District Nurses' Home in Springclose Lane.

Although there is nothing in either of these views to indicate their location, living memory and personal knowledge is still available to identify the present-day location as the housing development in Springclose Lane.

Love Lane, c.1912. The wooden gateposts stand at the rear entrance to the house called 'The Quarry', which stood where the angle of Quarry Park Road is now.

The old, rural atmosphere has been wiped out by the modern bypass road, but the two gateposts can still be seen, leading to the rear of the modern house in the corner of Quarry Park Road.

The Red Lion public house in Park Road in about 1920. In earlier days it had given its name to the highway - Red Lion Street.

No comment is needed here, as the photographs speak for themselves.

A good view of Cheam Brewery on the corner of Ewell Road and Malden Road. The ever-present representative of the police has his back to The Plough public house, and the narrow lane straight ahead is Ewell Road. The posters on the wall tell us that it is 1920, and that the brewery is about to be demolished and second-hand building materials will be for sale (as also shown on page 14).

Not only the brewery, but all the other buildings in the old picture have gone.

Ewell Road in 1921, looking eastwards, with The Plough public house visible at the crossroads, and the brewery on the left-hand side. On the right is the high brick wall of Cheam Court Farm, on top of which peacocks could frequently be seen.

The kerb-line is almost identical with that in the old view, all the road-widening having taken place on the left-hand side in the early 1920s.

A view of Station Way looking towards the crossroads, with the farm buildings of Cheam Court Farm on the left, and cottages and one small shop on the right.

On the left, the shops, with flats above, replaced the farm buildings in 1933; but the cottages on the right, now converted to shops, are still recognisable.

The Century Cinema, standing in Station Way on the corner of Kingsway Road, in 1938. It closed in 1960, and the frontage was demolished; but the main auditorium was not pulled down until 1990, when the whole site was redeveloped.

Both sides of the street beyond the cinema site are recognisable, having changed little over the last fifty years.

Cheam Station Approach from Upper Mulgrave Road in 1975, when it was flanked with lock-up shops.

The station building is recognisable in both views, rendering any further identification unnecessary. it is interesting that both photographs were taken by the same photographer.

A rare picture of The Plough public house across the foot of High Street, looking into Station Way.

Our friend the policeman very obviously replaced here by traffic signals, which were installed in 1938.